IMAGES OF SPORT

NORWICH
SPEEDWAY

IMAGES OF SPORT

NORWICH
SPEEDWAY

NORMAN JACOBS & MIKE KEMP

TEMPUS

Dedicated to the memory of Fred Rogers.

Frontispiece: Fred Rogers, Norwich 1948-1954.

First published 2004

Tempus Publishing Limited
The Mill, Brimscombe Port,
Stroud, Gloucestershire, GL5 2QG
www.tempus-publishing.com

© Norman Jacobs & Mike Kemp, 2004

British Library Cataloguing in Publication Data.
A catalogue record for this book is available from the British Library.

ISBN 0 7524 3152 8

Typesetting and origination by Tempus Publishing Limited.
Printed in Great Britain by Midway Colour Print, Wiltshire.

Contents

An aerial view of the Firs taken in 1932, shortly after the opening of the grandstand. Note the country setting.

Acknowledgements

The authors would like to thank Keith Farman for his kind permission in allowing us to use the fruits of his research, particularly on the early days at Norwich, as well as a number of photographs.

All other illustrations are from Mike Kemp's own collection.

Foreword

It was 1954 – the first time I came to Norwich and the first time I saw the Firs speedway stadium. In the run-up to the World Championship, through rounds in Scandinavia and on the continent, I had qualified for the 'champion rounds' in the UK.

My draw was for Norwich and West Ham. I can remember taking a train from London Liverpool Street station, wheeling my bike on to a goods wagon, getting on board and travelling to Norwich. At Thorpe station I was met by the Stars' captain, Aub Lawson. I didn't know him. As a matter of fact, I had never even heard of him at the time.

Aub brought me and my bike to the stadium – he was very kind and tried to make me feel welcome. I must have been very frightened and nervous, coming from a small town in Sweden to England for the first time on my own. I had only been to 'the home of speedway racing' once before with a touring Swedish team. I did not understand much English, and spoke even less, and yet here I was, at the start of my biggest adventure. But once on the speedway bike I was on my own and I knew I wanted to show what I could do. The track was very much like most Swedish tracks and I found my way around quite easily. At the end of the day, to my surprise, I finished runner-up. I was so happy, and, of course, I loved the Firs. You always love a track where you do well. I also managed to ride well at West Ham, so the road to Wembley was open for my first world final.

During the winter of 1954-1955, I toured Australia and again met up with Aub Lawson. By now I knew what a great speedway rider and gentleman he was. Aub asked me if I might be interested in riding for the Norwich Stars, and I just jumped for joy. This was the chance every rider dreamed about, especially me, to ride in the English First Division and at a track I knew and liked. So when the boat from Australia docked in England I travelled with Aub to Norwich, the place which was to become my home for the next eleven years; years I loved and enjoyed. It was a very sad day for me when I was told that the stadium was sold and there would be no more speedway. I have been back to look at the site where the stadium used to be and I felt a little bitter and angry that a place that brought so much happiness to so many people had to be destroyed. I quite often return to Norwich. I love the city and the Norfolk people and still think of it as my second home. When I retired it was my intention to live in Norfolk, but it was not to be.

When my good friend Mike Kemp asked me to write a few words for a book on Norwich speedway he was working on with the well-known writer of speedway books Norman Jacobs, I felt honoured but at the same time a little nervous: it is one thing to ride a speedway machine and quite another to write the foreword to a book! One thing I'm sure of is that when two speedway historians like Mike and Norman get together it will be a success. I'm very much looking forward to seeing some of the several hundred speedway pictures Mike has, and the story Norman will tell. Hopefully you, dear reader, will enjoy the book as much as I'm sure I will – it's bound to bring back so many memories.

Happy reading and kind regards, Ove.

Ove Fundin

June 2003

Ove Fundin, Norwich 1955-1964.

The Stars through the Years

Pioneering Days

On Sunday 17 August 1930, a crowd, reported to be in the region of 5,000, turned up to see the first meeting held at the Firs Stadium, Aylsham Road, Norwich. The first race was the one-mile scratch race, and was won by Jack Newlands. Other riders to appear at Norwich's first meeting, organised by Don Hannent on behalf of the Eastern Speedways Motor Club, included Bill Butler and G. Middleton.

Speedway had first seen the light of day in this country on 19 February 1928 at High Beech in Essex. So popular did the sport become that by the end of 1928 speedway tracks had sprung up all over the country from Brighton to Edinburgh and from Cardiff to Bradford. In 1929 two leagues were introduced, and in 1930, the first Test match between England and Australia was held at Wimbledon. Therefore, in comparison to many other places, Norwich was quite late in succumbing to this new craze.

But succumb it did, as the meeting on 17 August proved so popular that a follow-up was held just less than one month later on 14 September. Unfortunately, the organisers had picked the wrong day as the heavens opened and it poured with rain. A contemporary report said that 'the riders carried on pluckily under the difficult conditions and some good sport, considering the conditions, was seen.' Not surprisingly the number of spectators was well down, with only 1,000 braving the elements.

This meeting brought the season to a close, but 4,000 fans attended on 26 April 1931 to see the first meeting of the new year. Rain again affected the proceedings, but not Jack Newlands as he once more proved victorious in the one-mile race on his Grindley Peerless.

The next meeting, on 24 May 1931, saw Jack Newlands change his name to 'Speedy Jack'. Change of name or not, he once again won the one-mile race. Changes of name became popular at the Firs as Fred Leavis became Arthur Reynolds, while others not to use their real names included Allen Kilfoyle, known at the Firs as Jack Williams, and Australian Test rider Jack Sharp, known as Jack Smythe.

By the time of the next meeting, on 14 June, all riders had been given their own number which they wore on their back so that supporters could identify them. 'Speedy Jack' was number 1 while Arthur Reynolds was number 9.

Racing continued on a regular basis throughout 1931 in front of crowds regularly numbering 5,000-6,000. By July, seating for 500 had been provided.

Until now, the Firs was really a grass track rather than a proper speedway. By September, however, the grass had been so worn away that big clouds of dust were thrown up as the riders cornered, and it became noticeable that the riders who broadsided round the corners were faster and more spectacular than those who didn't. It was therefore decided to turn the Firs into a proper dirt track to make the racing more exciting.

The first proper dirt-track meeting at the Firs was held on 13 September 1931 and was a challenge match between Norwich and Staines held in front of a crowd of over 6,000. The Norwich team for this match, and therefore Norwich's first-ever team, was Arthur Reynolds (captain), George Francis (vice-captain), Herb Peters, Bert Linn, Johnny Bull and Joe Nelson with Jack Williams, Les Warboys and Don Dimes as reserves. The match was won by Norwich 33-21.

The following week Staines returned for a second match and this time they ran out winners by a single point, 27-26. In the last heat Johnny Bull broke a chain one-and-a-quarter laps from the finishing line and started to push home for a point. Unfortunately he quickly tired, resorted to a tow, and was disqualified. Had he managed to push home the result would have been a draw.

By the end of the 1931 season, crowds had grown to over 7,000 as Norwich fans quickly took team racing to their hearts. Following the two matches against Staines, Norwich lost to Cambridge, beat Dagenham and then drew with Cambridge, who were making a return visit.

Over the close season, the track was completely relaid and a new safety fence erected. A new stand was also partially finished in time for the opening meeting, seating 600. Nearly 8,000 watched the opening match on 27 March 1932, a team match against 'London'. The 1,200 seat grandstand was completed in time for the second meeting on 10 April.

On 1 May, Norwich took on a proper league team for the first time when they entertained Lea Bridge, winning 33-14. The seventeen-year-old Geoff Pymar turned out for the home team for the first time. The following week, Pymar lowered the one-lap track record to 21.2 seconds.

Racing in front of large crowds continued on a regular basis throughout 1932 and climaxed with a night-time meeting on 22 October at which the track illumination was augmented by extra-powerful arc lights.

The Firs reopened for the 1933 season on 2 April. A major breakthrough came on 25 June when, for the first time, speedway racing in Norwich was held under an ACU permit. The occasion was a special Australian Riders v. The Rest challenge match. Advertised to appear in the Australian line-up were two men who were later to play a major role at the Firs; Dick Wise, who scored four points, and Max Grosskreutz, who, in the event, seems not to have ridden, possibly due to illness.

The ACU permit led to a number of top stars appearing at Norwich during 1933, including Tiger Hart, Dicky Case, Stan Greatrex and Stew Fairbairn. Geoff Pymar also rode, having by now joined Wimbledon. For the meeting on 7 October he was billed as 'The local boy and team-mate of Vic Huxley of Wimbledon.'

Perversely, although the bigger names had started to appear, the crowds had fallen and for the next three years there was no speedway at the Firs apart from one appearance of Putt Mossman's American stunt troupe in 1936.

The Max Grosskreutz Years

Speedway racing returned to the Firs in 1937 under the direction of former Belle Vue and Australia star Max Grosskreutz. The Norwich Stars entered the newly formed Provincial League and started off their campaign with a National Trophy match at home to Liverpool on 1 May. The team for that historic encounter (points in brackets) was skipper Dick Wise (5), Wilf Jay (8), Alan Smith (4), Jim Millward (6), Jock Sweet (3), Charlie Lish (0), Charlie Dugard (2) and Paul Goodchild (2).

Unfortunately it was not a happy introduction to the big time as they lost by 30 points to 51. They went on to lose eleven of their next thirteen matches as well. The turning point in Norwich's first season came at the beginning of June, when Norwich signed up the leg-trailing Australian Bert Spencer, on loan from Wimbledon, as captain. He was the inspiration behind the league win on 19 June against Liverpool, scoring 17 points and breaking the track record, setting up a time of 78.2 seconds, a whole second faster than the previous record. From then on the team's fortunes improved a little though they still finished the season sixth out of seven teams.

The one encouraging aspect, however, was the numbers of people coming to watch the team. By the end of the season, 9,000 spectators was not uncommon.

In 1938, the Provincial League officially became the National League Second Division. With Bert Spencer's recall to Wimbledon at the end of 1937, things did not start too well for Norwich, with three wins and four losses. However, the season was completely transformed on 14 May in the match against Southampton, when, firstly, Spencer returned and secondly, Grosskreutz himself decided to come out of retirement to help his team. Grosskreutz showed he had lost none of his skill as he scored 9 points from his first three rides and then, having ensured victory for the Stars, stood down in his last ride.

Thanks to the inspirational Grosskreutz, Norwich pulled off the sensation of the season by beating First Division Harringay in the National Trophy. Harringay was packed with big names, including Jack and Norman Parker, Alec Statham, Jack Ormston and Les Wotton. It was the first time a Second Division team had beaten a First Division team in an official fixture.

The former Australian Test star and Belle Vue Ace Max Grosskreutz was manager of Norwich from 1937-1939.

At the end of the season, Norwich tied with Hackney Wick for first place, but lost out on the title because they had scored less race points.

During 1938, the Firs was considered to be the fastest track in the country, but over the close season the ACU ruled that less cinders were to be used, and at the start of 1939 this led to slower times. In an effort to improve times, Grosskreutz relaid the track with a special granite preparation of the sort used on tracks in his native Australia. It proved to be a success and times improved once again.

The season began well for the Stars as they defeated league champions Hackney Wick, 46-38. Grosskreutz decided it was safe to retire again as he was sure that his top riders, Spencer, Wal Morton, Wilf Jay and Dick Wise could maintain Norwich's challenge for league honours. Unfortunately the season ended prematurely due to the outbreak of the Second World War.

The Dick Wise Years

Norwich Stars reopened after the Second World War on 20 April 1946 with a challenge match against Sheffield. The team had joined the newly-formed Northern League, and the new manager was former Norwich rider Dick Wise. Bert Spencer and Wilf Jay returned to the Firs and were joined by Ted Bravery, Paddy Mills, Sid Hipperson, Don Houghton, Albert Hutson and Harwood Pike. During the season, Roy Duke, Charlie Challis, Len Read, Bluey Thorpe and Paddy Hammond signed for the team.

The immediate post-war years were the boom years for speedway and Norwich saw its gates double from pre-war days, with an average attendance of almost 20,000 in 1946. The track was still one of the longest in the country at 425 yards.

The first post-war season saw Norwich lift their first trophies when the Stars took the Northern Trophy, beating Sheffield in the final by 106 points to 85, and the ACU Cup (Northern). At the end of 1946 Wilf Jay left the Firs, having been involved with the club since 1937, to be replaced by Syd Littlewood, an Australian, but now domiciled in Norwich, who had ridden for the club in 1938.

The following year, the leagues were reorganised into the National League First, Second and Third Divisions; Norwich joining the Second Division. The Stars mounted a serious challenge on league honours in 1947, but an injury to Bert Spencer affected the team and they finished in third place. Phil Clarke took his place in the team while Paddy Mills became the Stars' leading rider.

Speedway's popularity was probably now at its peak, and with 460,000 people passing through the turnstiles in 1947, the accommodation was extended to hold 26,000 spectators.

1948 saw Bert Spencer injured again, and Norwich dropped to fifth place in the league. The only real success came in reaching the Second Division final of the National Trophy, but they were defeated in both legs by Birmingham. In spite of this indifferent season, Norwich applied to join the First Division but their application was turned down.

Bristol totally dominated the Second Division in 1949 with Norwich and Sheffield fighting it out for the runner-up spot. Although Norwich managed to beat Bristol at

Dick Wise, who had captained Norwich in their pre-war days, managed the Stars from 1946-1949.

home, they inexplicably lost to Cradley Heath to finish the season in third place. Once again the Stars reached the National Trophy Second Division final. This time they put up a better show, just losing out to Bristol 111–105 on aggregate, having won the home leg by 76 points to 32, Phil Clarke scoring an 18-point maximum.

After missing even more matches due to yet another injury, Spencer decided it was time to call it a day and at the end of the season he returned to Australia. With Dick Wise also leaving at the end of the 1949 season, it meant that Norwich had severed its last links with the pre-war team.

The Fred Evans Years

The new manager at Norwich was the former Birmingham and Hackney Wick manager Fred Evans. He moulded the experience of Paddy Mills and Ted Bravery with the newer Stars, Phil Clarke, Fred Rogers, Johnny Davies and the Australian Bob Leverenz, into a championship-winning team. With the promotion of Bristol to the First Division, the league took on a much more competitive air, with any one of four or five teams in the running for the title, but in the end it was Norwich who came out on top in 1950.

At the end of the previous two seasons, the winners and runners-up of the Second Division, Birmingham and Bristol, had been promoted to the First Division, so Norwich put in their application and waited. Unfortunately, the London clubs voted against their promotion as they said that their experience of visits from provincial teams was far from a happy one as the gates invariably fell.

Fred Evans was determined to show the speedway world what a mistake it had made in not promoting Norwich, saying that if the London clubs would not let the Stars into the First Division, 'we'll smash our way in!' And smash their way in they did as they romped away with the league title in 1951 by 10 clear points. In the process they repeated their pre-war success of beating First Division opposition in the National Trophy. This time it was Bristol who felt the full force of the Norwich onslaught. It was impossible to ignore their application for First Division status after this. Bob Leverenz was the star of the team, averaging over 10 points per match and qualifying for the World Championship final, where he came ninth.

As it turned out, maybe it would have been better if they had not been promoted after all, as 1952 turned out to be a disastrous year for the Stars. They finished bottom of the First Division with just one away win to their credit. Ironically, they also suffered the ignominy of being beating in the National Trophy by a Second Division team, Poole.

Only Leverenz and new signing Bill Gilbert (a former Wembley rider) were able to live in the new division. In fact, Leverenz managed to retain his 10-point average, one of only three riders in the league to record a double figure average, the others being Ronnie Moore and Jack Young.

Fred Evans took over the managerial reins in 1950 and remained as manager until 1954. Before the Second World War, Evans had been manager of Norwich's arch-rivals Hackney Wick Wolves, as well as Birmingham Hall Green.

Just as it seemed as though things could not get any worse for Norwich, both Leverenz and Gilbert announced their retirements; Leverenz midway through the season and Gilbert at the end.

Fortunately, Evans was able to entice former West Ham star Aub Lawson back to this country after a year's absence in his native Australia, and Cyril Roger was signed up from the now-defunct New Cross. But, even so, 1953 was not much better than 1952 and the team finished the season with just 12 points from sixteen matches. Incredibly, two clubs, Belle Vue and Bristol, had even worse seasons, finishing below them in the league.

There was a marked improvement from the Stars in 1954 as former world number three Bob Oakley was signed up, and Aub Lawson returned to something like the form that had taken him to second place in the world rankings in 1950. Norwich moved up the table to finish in a respectable fourth place, and also reached the final of the National Trophy, losing to Wembley 123-92.

But 1954 was to prove to be probably the most significant year in Norwich's history for a very different reason, as it heralded the first appearance at the Firs of a young Swede by the name of Ove Fundin. The unknown Fundin, riding on a bike held together with bits of old wire and string, scored 13 points to finish runner-up to Aub Lawson in the Norwich round of the World Championship. Lawson was most impressed, and when he saw how well he performed in Australia over the close season, he contacted the new Norwich manager Gordon Parkins, recommending he sign this youngster from Tranas immediately before anyone else snapped him up.

The Gordon Parkins Years

1955 saw Norwich take their first senior title when they carried off the National Trophy, reversing the result of the previous year's final by defeating the powerful Wembley Lions. Unfortunately it was not such a good year in the league, as, partly due to injuries to Aub Lawson, who twice broke his collarbone, the team struggled and eventually finished just 1 point above West Ham at the foot of the table. The bright spot of the league season was the form of new boy Ove Fundin. Joining late in the season, he rode in just six matches but still managed to score 73 points. In the National Trophy final he scored 16 points in the away leg.

It was a good year individually for the Stars as no less than four of them, Fundin, Clarke, Roger and Lawson, qualified for the World Championship final and when Lawson's broken collarbone forced him to withdraw from the event, his place was taken by yet another Norwich rider, Billy Bales.

There were a number of new names in the Stars' line-up for 1956 as Gerry Hussey, Reg Trott, Peter Atkins, Derek Strutt and that veteran of the pioneer days at the Firs, Geoff Pymar, all joined the team. To make way for them, Cyril Roger and Don Lawson, Aub's half-brother, left. Hussey proved to be the pick of the newcomers, scoring 63 points from ten matches and qualifying for the World Championship final.

Ove Fundin continued his phenomenal rise to the top of the speedway tree, taking the World Championship at Wembley on 22 September for the first of his record-breaking five wins.

As for the Stars, they had a middling year, finishing in fourth place in a league of seven teams, having drawn no less than four of their matches, with another four being decided on a 43-41 scoreline. Their National Trophy success of the previous year was not to be repeated as the team went out 96-120 to eventual winners Wimbledon in the semi-final.

With Wembley and Poole closing prior to the start of the 1957 season, it was decided to amalgamate the two divisions of the National League into just one comprising twelve teams. It meant that, for the first time, Norwich and local rivals Ipswich were in the same league.

Gordon Parkins, photographed here holding the National Trophy won by Norwich in 1955, was Norwich's last manager, looking after the team from 1955-1964. Pictured with him in the front row are, from left to right: Fred Brand, Les Mullins, Gordon Parkins, Malcolm Flood, Billy Bales, Phil Clarke, Harry Edwards, Aub Lawson, Cyril Roger, Don Lawson.

It looked at the start of 1957 as though the Stars might have their first success in a league competition as they topped their section of the Britannia Cup. With petrol rationing being introduced to Britain as a result of the 1956 Suez crisis, the Promoters' Association had decided to start the season with a regionalised competition to cut down on travelling costs. Norwich won the southern section against Wimbledon, Southampton, Ipswich and Swindon, while Belle Vue were victorious in the northern section. The top two teams met over a two-legged contest to decide the fate of the trophy. The first leg was held at Belle Vue, where the Stars managed to force a 48-48 draw and it looked odds-on that Norwich would take the title back at the Firs, but some brilliant riding by Peter Craven, Ron Johnston and Bob Duckworth saw the Aces through 50-46 on the night and 98-94 on aggregate.

Although it was a surprise home loss that lost Norwich their chance of a trophy, it was their poor away form that prevented them from doing better in the league, as they remained in fourth place. Lawson and Fundin both had outstanding years, recording averages of 13.67 and 12.4 respectively.

The brilliant form of Lawson and Fundin continued in 1958. Although by now Fundin had staked his claim to be the best rider in the world, Lawson's claim to be considered among the world's elite was probably, in some ways, even more remarkable. One of the few pre-war riders still riding – he had first come to Britain in 1939 – he was still averaging 11.63. Even more amazingly, he managed, for the first time in his career and nineteen years after he had first qualified, to grab a tractor ride at Wembley, finishing third in the World Championship final, one place behind his younger teammate Ove Fundin.

With strong backing from Billy Bales, Phil Clarke and newcomer to the side, pint-sized Australian Johnny Chamberlain, Norwich had their best season so far in the senior league, finishing as runners-up. They were also runners-up in the National Trophy, once again losing out to Belle Vue in a major final; though this time they were beaten in both legs. In particular, Peter Craven was in spectacular form for the Aces and pulled off the almost unheard of feat of beating Ove Fundin twice in the Firs leg.

1959 saw Norwich as East Anglia's sole surviving speedway team in senior league racing after the withdrawal of Ipswich from the National League, although near-neighbours Yarmouth entered the Southern Area League. It wasn't such a good year for the Stars as they dropped down the league to finish in fourth place, their poor away form having cost them the chance to consolidate their position as one of the best two teams in the league. It was somewhat ironic that, after the events of the previous two years, their only away victory came at Belle Vue. Norwich reached the semi-final of the National Trophy, going out by the disappointing margin of 40 points, 128-88, to Southampton. Both Fundin and Lawson continued to contribute 10-plus averages for all matches during the season.

For the first time since 1947, Norwich lined up for the following season without Phil Clarke. With the Firs veteran leaving the line-up, a new name was added to the team sheet for 1960 when a seventeen-year-old youngster by the name of Terry Betts came to the fore. Betts was destined to remain associated with Norfolk teams Norwich and King's Lynn for an even longer period than Phil Clarke, as, after Norwich's closure in 1964, Betts turned out for King's Lynn from 1965 to 1978. His start for Norwich, however, gave little hint of what was in store for Betts as, in all, he rode four times for the Stars and failed to score a single point.

1960 was to be another average year for the Stars as they finished fifth in the league. Once again Fundin and Lawson dominated proceedings. As usual, they did better in the National Trophy, this time reaching the final for the second time in three years, and the fourth time in the last six it had been held. Unfortunately, Norwich were once again destined to finish runners-up, as they lost to Wimbledon by 115 to 104 on aggregate.

But it was the semi-final against the old enemy Belle Vue that really set the terraces alight at the Firs. After the first leg in Manchester, Norwich trailed by 24 points and very few people gave the Stars a chance of pulling back that sort of deficit, but after a run of four heats starting with heat seven, in which Norwich scored three 5-1s and a 4-2, the impossible began to look a little more possible. There were now eight heats left with the aggregate score standing at Belle Vue 89 Norwich 79. Craven stopped the rot for the Aces by winning heat eleven but Lawson and Bales combined for another 5-1 in heat thirteen. Disaster struck in heat fourteen as Belle Vue's Slant Payling lost control of his machine on the second lap and somersaulted into the fence. Following close behind, his teammate, Derek 'Tink' Maynard, had no chance of avoiding the fallen rider and bike and crashed into the wreckage. Payling was excluded and Maynard was unable to take part in the rerun, having been rushed to hospital. A 5-0 to Norwich meant they were now only three points behind.

At the end of heat 17 the scores were Belle Vue 105 Norwich 103. Norwich nominated Fundin and Chamberlain for the final heat, while Belle Vue tracked Peter Craven and Ron Johnston. Chamberlain felt that Bales should be given the second spot and stood down from the race. As the tapes rose, Fundin shot off into the lead but Bales was badly boxed and came out of the first turn in last place. With Craven in full pursuit of Fundin, Bales saw his opportunity to get past Johnston and with the crowd going crazy and yelling their heads off, Bales managed to inch his way into third place. Meanwhile, up front, Fundin and Craven were engaged in a neck-and-neck duel as Craven got his wheel in front of Fundin, only for Fundin to fight his way back and to eventually win one of the best races ever seen at the Firs. The resulting 4-2 for the Stars meant that the semi-final was tied on 107 each.

Unfortunately there was a tragic epilogue to what had been this most exciting of matches when it was announced that 'Tink' Maynard had succumbed to his head injuries and had died in the early hours of the following morning.

In the rerun, Norwich made no mistake as they took a 14-point lead at the Firs and then won the second leg by 55 points to 53 in a rain-affected match at Hyde Road.

In the four semi-final matches, Fundin had scored two maximum 18s plus two 17s. In the final against Wimbledon he was to score another 18 and another 17. Fundin easily topped that year's National League and Trophy score charts with an incredible average of 16.00. His total points score of 448 (without a single bonus point!) was the highest in the league, three more than Peter Craven in spite of riding in four fewer matches. Fundin went on to crown what was arguably his best season ever by winning the World Championship for the second time.

Lawson did not return for the 1961 season as his wife had become seriously ill back home in Australia and he decided he needed to stay with her. His loss left Norwich very weak with Fundin the only home rider to finish the season in the top twenty of the National League averages with the result that the team dropped to seventh place in the league, winning just seven matches out of the eighteen raced. Incredibly, however, Norwich's known cup-fighting qualities came to the fore again when they knocked the mighty Wimbledon Dons out of the National Trophy in the second round after taking a 20-point lead in the home leg. This was one of only four matches Wimbledon lost in the whole League and Trophy season. Unfortunately, the Stars could not sustain their success and they went out to Swindon in the semi-final.

The 1962 season got off to an unfortunate start as the opening meeting on 31 March had to be abandoned following a heavy snowfall. Things didn't get a lot better once it did start as both Fundin and Bales were injured, and this badly affected the Stars' chances of picking up any honours. Olle Nygren and Gote Nordin were called in as short-term replacements and did well enough, but they were not the great Ove Fundin. The revelation of the season was Terry Betts. Since his induction into the team in 1960, his progress with the Stars had been very slow, but all that was to change on the night of 14 July when Norwich visited Belle Vue. On a night when Fundin was to score just 4 points, Betts trounced Peter Craven twice on his way to recording a faultless 15-point maximum. By the end of the season, Betts had established himself as the number two at the Firs and never looked back. But it was not a good season for the team and they finished in fifth place out of seven teams.

Nygren had made such a good impression on his few outings with the Stars that Gordon Parkins wanted to sign him up permanently for 1963. Unfortunately, he found he couldn't, as this would contravene the Speedway Riders' Association policy of allowing only one foreign rider per team. With a team now consisting of Fundin, Betts, John Debbage, Reg Trott, Jimmy Gooch, youngster Trevor Hedge and the injured Billy Bales, Parkins felt the team was far too weak to compete in the National League and considered withdrawing. If this happened there would be just six teams left and the Control Board felt this to be unviable; so they stepped in, and following negotiations between them, Parkins and the SRA, it was agreed that Nygren could sign after all.

The programme cover from the meeting held on 16 April 1933. 6,000 spectators saw former Lea Bridge star Reg Stanley win the final of the Stadium Handicap, beating Reynolds into third place.

Nygren's arrival transformed the Stars and they had their best-ever season, finishing runners-up to Belle Vue and winning the National Trophy, beating Belle Vue in the final. Fundin continued to carry all before him and won the World Championship for the fourth time.

Fundin and Nygren continued to dominate the proceedings in 1964 and with Sandor Levai and Trevor Hedge both getting better and better as the season went on, it was another successful season for the Stars, although they dropped one place to third in the league.

Although it was a reasonably successful season on the track, it was most certainly not a successful season for the supporters, as during the season, it was announced that the Firs Stadium was to be sold for redevelopment, and that therefore there would be no speedway after the end of the 1964 season. It came as a complete shock to the fans, although the riders had known for some time that the axe might fall.

The last meeting was held on 31 October 1964. A number of former Stars put in an appearance, including Jack Freeman, Phil Clarke, Wilf Jay and Lennie Read. At the end of the meeting Cyril Crane took hold of the PA system and told the management what he thought of them for selling out. Since that time Crane has made many attempts to bring speedway back to the city, but all have proved unsuccessful, though he did, of course, revive the Stars name at King's Lynn the following year.

Phil Clarke holds the record for both the most appearances in Norwich colours (309) and the highest number of points scored (2162). For appearances he is followed by Billy Bales on 245; Jack Freeman, 190; Paddy Mills, 181 and Fred Rogers, 176. For points, he is followed by Ove Fundin, 1862; Billy Bales, 1580; Aub Lawson, 1347 and Paddy Mills, 1360.5.

two

The Early Years, 1930-1936

Riders getting ready for the start of the one-mile Scratch Race at the first meeting held at the Firs on 17 August 1930. The race was won by J. Newlands (far right), second was W. Littleboy (second left) and third was G. Middleton (first left). Perhaps it was inevitable that Newlands should have won as he is the only one wearing leathers!

The line-up for the final of the one-mile event at the second meeting, held on 14 September 1930. This was won by Bill Butler, third from the right.

A close-up photograph of Bill Butler on his Douglas, taken in what passed for the pits at Norwich's second meeting. As well as the one-mile event, Butler also won the two-mile race in a time of 4 minutes 51.5 seconds.

The Grand Parade of riders at the meeting held on 14 June 1931. The parade is being led by top local star, 'Speedy Jack' (No.1). Also in the photograph are Bill Butler (far right), Arthur Reynolds (second right) and George Rowney (fourth right). Arthur Reynolds won the afternoon's Two-Mile Handicap event, while 'Speedy Jack' won the One-Mile Handicap for local riders.

Two photographs of Johnny Bull in action. Bull seems to have adopted a strange style of cornering, preferring to keep his leg in the air. Along with Arthur Reynolds, Bull rode in Norwich's first-ever team which rode against Staines on 13 September 1931.

Geoff Pymar, a local lad from Diss, first rode at the Firs at the second meeting on 14 September 1930. He was included in the Norwich team for the first time on 1 May 1932. He made such an impression that he was given a trial by Wimbledon, and soon made the team, partnering the great Vic Huxley. Pymar went on to ride in six Test matches for England and qualify for the 1938 World Championship final.

The Australian Jack Sharp came to Britain in 1931 to ride for High Beech. He also rode several times for Norwich under the assumed name of Jack Smythe. In 1933 he was appointed captain of Plymouth and in 1934 he went on to ride for Wimbledon and become an Australian Test rider.

Yet another Wimbledon rider to ride for the Norwich team was Fred Leavis, who rode under the name of Arthur Reynolds. Reynolds was captain of that historic first Norwich team and continued as skipper until the end of the 1932 season. Along with Jack Sharp, Leavis took part in the Australian Riders *v.* The Rest match on 25 June 1933. This was the first match held at the Firs under ACU licence, as a consequence of which Sharp and Leavis were able to use their real names. Sharp scored 4 for the Australians, while Leavis scored 7 for The Rest.

Racing came to a virtual halt at Norwich at the end of the 1933 season, but in 1936, Putt Mossman's Rodeo and Circus put on a meeting at the Firs. Putt Mossman's troupe toured the country during the 1930s putting on racing and speciality acts at many provincial circuits. It is said that Mossman helped to save some tracks from extinction, including Southampton, Plymouth and Bristol, with the crowds he brought in. Maybe it was his appearance at the Firs that helped towards Norwich's renaissance the following year…

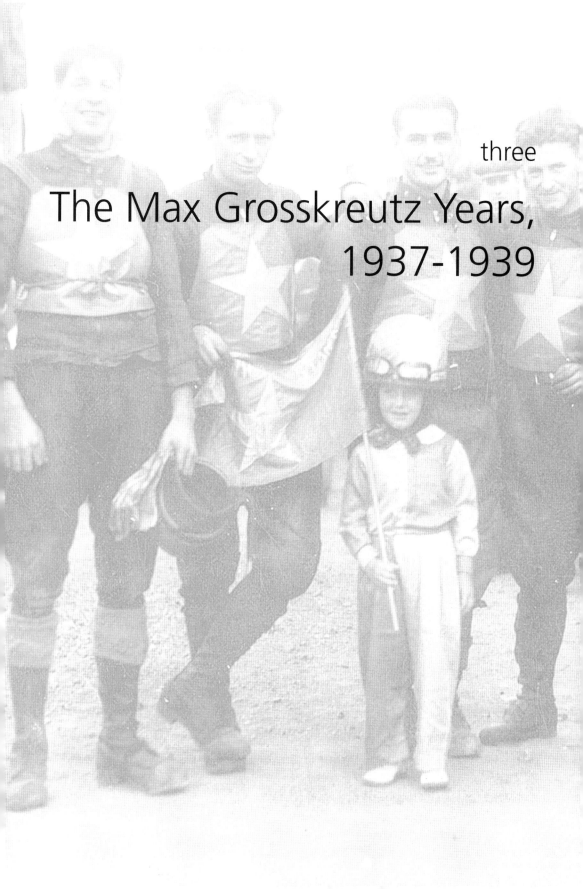

three

The Max Grosskreutz Years, 1937-1939

The 1937 Norwich team. From left to right: Jock Sweet, Alec Peel, James McMahon (promoter), Max Grosskreutz, Dick Wise (Captain, on bike), Wilf Jay, Paul Goodchild, Bill Birtwell, Bert Spencer.

Bert Spencer in 1937 Norwich colours. Spencer was an Australian who began his racing career in 1927 at Brisbane. He came to England in 1928 as a member of A.J. Hunting's International Speedway Ltd group of riders. In 1929 he rode for Exeter, moving on to Leicester Super in 1930 and Plymouth in 1931, with whom he stayed until 1934. He rode in America in 1935 and in 1936 came back to England to ride for Wimbledon. He was signed on loan for Norwich in June 1937.

Spencer was one of the most spectacular riders ever seen on British speedway tracks as this leg-trailing action shot confirms. He was the mainstay of the Norwich team throughout the 1937–1939 period, although he missed a short period at the start of 1938 before transferring full time from Wimbledon.

Opposite above: Spencer returned to Norwich after the Second World War and rode for the Stars from 1946 to 1949. He carried on with the leg-trailing style even though most of the rest of the world had moved on to foot forward. This did not stop his prolific scoring, however, and in 1946 he topped the Northern League averages, scoring 200 points from twenty matches. This photograph shows him in action against Sheffield. From left to right the riders are: Tommy Allott, Syd Littlewood, Len Williams and Bert Spencer.

Opposite below: He also qualified for the final of the British Riders' Championship in 1946, ridden that year in place of the World Championship, scoring 5 points to finish in tenth place. Although dogged by injury in his last few years he remained a leading scorer with the club. His last meeting was on 24 September 1949 when he scored 10 points against Glasgow.

Above right: Wal Morton rode for Norwich during the three pre-war league years. Born in Birmingham, Morton started his career at Coventry before moving on to West Ham and Wimbledon. He returned to Norwich after the Second World War, riding for the Stars in 1948 and again in 1957.

Below right: Although Scottish by birth, former grass-track rider Jock Sweet first rode on cinders in Australia during the 1936/37 season. In 1937 he joined Norwich and stayed with the team until the outbreak of the Second World War. He was once asked if he had any superstitions, and he replied that before coming to Norwich his main superstition was wearing anything green or yellow!

Left: Wilf Jay started his speedway career at Belle Vue in 1936 and came to Norwich with Grosskreutz in 1937, helping the latter build the new track. He was an immediate success, winning his first race and four out of six altogether at his first meeting. He finished the season as Norwich's top scorer. He returned to Norwich after the Second World War.

Below: The 1938 Norwich team. From left to right: Wilf Jay, Bill Birtwell, Max Grosskreutz, Wal Morton, Bert Spencer, Dick Wise, Paul Goodchild, Jock Sweet.

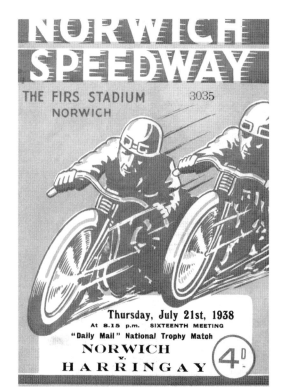

The programme cover from the famous National Trophy match held on 21 July 1938. It was the first time a team from the Second Division had beaten a team from the First Division in the National Trophy. The hero was, of course, Max Grosskreutz, who scored 17 paid 18 points.

The Firs returned to full-time speedway in 1937 under the direction of Australian international Max Grosskreutz. He laid a completely new cinder track and made a number of other improvements to the stadium. As well as manager, he was also the club's chief coach and mechanic. He returned to racing in 1938 and proved to be far too good for most of the National League Second Division, almost but not quite leading Norwich to victory in that league, the team losing out to Hackney Wick on race points.

Above left: Alan Smith was a local rider from Aylsham. He rode in Norwich's first league team and stayed for all three pre-war years, mainly as reserve.

Above right: Chun Moore had a very short career with the Stars, riding as a second string from May to July 1937.

A Norwich Speedway Supporters' Club card from 1938. 205,777 people passed through the Firs' turnstiles in 1938.

NORWICH SPEEDWAY SUPPORTERS CLUB, 1938

MEMBER'S TICKET

No. 1229

Name ....

Address .... 45 Beech Av.

.... Alvaston, Derby

Max Grosskreutz

Managing Director

Paul Goodchild's first experience of riding speedway was at Norwich in 1937. Previous to that he had, for six years, helped out at Belle Vue where he got to know Grosskreutz very well. He quickly showed great promise at the Firs and rode in the Stars' first match, scoring 2 points. He continued to score steadily as a second string, and in 1938 was included in England's 'Provincial' Test team against Australia. He stayed with Norwich until the outbreak of the Second World War.

Max Grosskreutz often returned to race in special events at his old club, Belle Vue. Here, he is shown shaking hands with the Belle Vue captain Eric Langton at the old Hyde Road track.

Opposite above: The 1939 Norwich team. From left to right: Alan Smith, Geoff Dukes (on bike), Keith Harvey, Bert Spencer, Wilf Jay, Max Grosskreutz, Wal Morton, Fred Strecker (on bike), Dick Wise. This photograph was taken in the Sheffield pits on 7 August 1939.

Opposite below left: Keith Harvey rode for Norwich in 1939, having transferred to the team following Crystal Palace's demise on 1 July of that year. His best performance came against Hackney Wick on 12 August when he scored 11.5 points.

Opposite below right: Fred Strecker also joined Norwich in 1939 following the collapse of his team, this time Stoke. The two points he gained in the last heat of his debut match against Bristol enabled the Stars to win an exciting match by just 1 point.

Right: An advertisement for Notwen Oil. These advertisements appeared in the Norwich programme during the 1939 season. Norwich captain Dick Wise was the Eastern Counties representative for Notwen.

Below: The cover of the Norwich Supporters' Club rulebook for 1938.

For trouble-free and economical motoring—*use*

NOTWEN

OIL

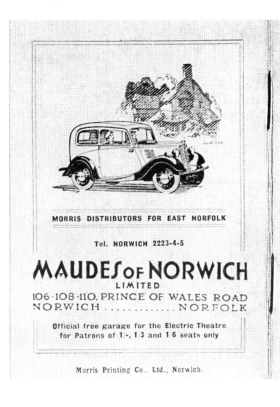

MORRIS DISTRIBUTORS FOR EAST NORFOLK

Tel. NORWICH 2223-4-5

MAUDES OF NORWICH
LIMITED
106·108·110, PRINCE OF WALES ROAD
NORWICH . . . . NORFOLK

Official free garage for the Electric Theatre for Patrons of 1/-, 1 3 and 1 6 seats only

Morris Printing Co., Ltd., Norwich.

NORWICH SPEEDWAY
SUPPORTERS' CLUB

RULES

Headquarters:
The Firs Stadium, Norwich

Dick Wise first took up speedway in his home town of Adelaide, South Australia, in 1927. He came to England in 1929 and rode at a number of tracks, including Sheffield, Stamford Bridge and Harringay, before settling at Norwich in 1937 as the team's first captain.

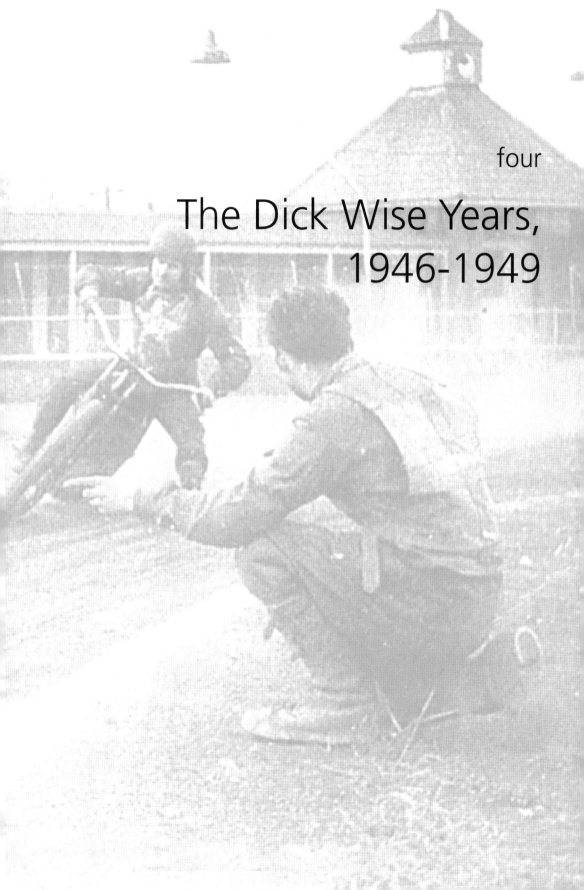

four

The Dick Wise Years,
1946-1949

The 1946 Norwich team. From left to right, back row: Ernie Howard (managing director), Syd Hipperson, Wilf Jay, Spud Murphy (track foreman), Charlie Challis, Len Read, Bluey Thorpe, Ted Bravery, Roy Duke, Harwood Pike, Dick Wise (manager). Front row: Paddy Mills, Bert Spencer (on bike), Paddy Hammond. Bert Spencer is holding the Northern Trophy, one of the two competitions won by Norwich in the first post-war season, the other being the ACU Cup (Northern).

Charlie Challis was a leg-trailer who had ridden for Birmingham and Crystal Palace pre-war. He made a number of appearances in the Norwich team in 1946 before being transferred to Plymouth in 1947.

Don Houghton was another member of the 1946 team, having ridden for Sheffield before the Second World War. He was transferred to Wigan at the start of the 1947 season.

Wilf Jay had just one more season at Norwich in 1946 before moving on to Newcastle. As well as winning his first race in the yellow and green of the Stars, he also won his last race in Stars' colours.

The cover of a booklet produced by Norwich to celebrate the 1946 season.

Opposite above: By the time he joined Norwich, Ted Bravery was already a veteran, having started out at Bristol in 1929. He seemed to find a new lease of life when he joined the Stars in 1946, scoring 136 points in his first season. On Wilf Jay's departure, he moved up to take the third-heat leader slot in 1947, but gradually age began to catch up on him, and he started to slide down the score charts. He was, however, always a first-class team man. He eventually retired at the end of the 1950 season.

Right: The programme cover for the first match of 1946, a challenge match against Sheffield. Norwich won the match 49-34.

Below: A 1949 Norwich speedway calendar.

A spectacular action shot from 1948, showing Syd Littlewood on the outside of Bert Spencer.

The 1947 Norwich team. From left to right, back row: Syd Littlewood, Ernie Howard, Jack Freeman, Ted Bravery, Geoff Revett, Roy Duke, Dick Wise. Front row: Paddy Hammond, Syd Hipperson, Bert Spencer (on bike), Paddy Mills.

The 1948 Norwich team. From left to right, back row: Phil Clarke, Aussie Powell, Jack Freeman, Geoff Revett, Bert Spencer, Ted Bravery. Front row: Syd Littlewood, Paddy Mills.

The 1949 Norwich team. From left to right: Phil Clarke, Ted Bravery, Fred Rogers, Syd Littlewood, Bob Leverenz, Bert Spencer, Alec Hunter, Jack Freeman. Inset in the background: Paddy Mills.

Left: One of the most popular riders ever to ride for Norwich, Paddy Mills had originally been discovered by Arthur Westwood and Bluey Wilkinson at Sheffield before the Second World War. Although he hadn't set the speedway world on fire, Dick Wise signed him up for Norwich at the start of the 1946 season. He immediately began to show his true class and finished the season as third-highest scorer with 153 points.

Below: He really came to the fore in the following two seasons as he topped the Norwich score chart in 1947 and 1948.

Opposite above: In 1949 he was all set to make his debut in the England Test team when an horrific accident put him out for several weeks. In a crash in June at Glasgow White City, Mills fractured his skull in three places, broke a leg and injured his face and eardrums. Many thought it would end Mills' career, but he was back in the saddle before the end of the season! Mills continued to ride for Norwich until 1952.

Paddy Mills was a top star at Norwich but was still willing to learn from his team-mates. Here, Billy Bales shows him how to ride the Yarmouth track.

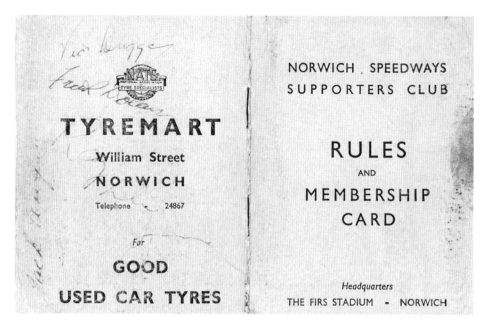

A 1947 Supporters' Club card. Norwich were averaging gates around 20,000 at this period.

Above left: Jack Freeman was born in Norwich and made his debut for the club in 1947 at the age of twenty-four. He remained with the Stars until 1952.

Above right: Paddy Hammond had his first taste of speedway in Germany during the Second World War. On his return to England in 1946 he signed up for Norwich. His scoring improved in 1947, but in 1948 he moved across to Yarmouth.

Geoff Revett had been discovered by Dicky Case at Rye House. He signed up for Norwich in 1946. Unfortunately his career was restricted by the fact that he could only ride in home meetings due to business commitments, though he stayed with the team until 1948.

Len Read, known as 'The Mighty Atom', first witnessed speedway at the old Firs Stadium back in 1930. When Max Grosskreutz arrived in 1937, Read had a few practice laps at the track under the watchful eye of Dick Wise and Syd Littlewood. He finally made the team in 1946 and remained until August 1947 when he transferred to Plymouth.

Harwood Pike was another pre-war Wilkinson discovery at Sheffield. He made his debut for Norwich midway through the 1946 season, finishing with a respectable total of 50 points. He was loaned out to Wombwell at the beginning of 1947. When Wombwell closed at the end of the 1948 season, Norwich sought his return but he went to Leicester instead.

Although he had something like twenty years of grass-track experience, Roy Duke did not take up speedway until he was in his mid-thirties, when he had a few practice laps at Dagenham in 1946, and then signed for Norwich. He had a bad accident in 1947 which resulted in a broken back. In 1948 he turned out for Yarmouth, but was transferred to Leicester in 1949.

Above left: The programme cover from Norwich's first meeting of the 1947 season, a challenge match against West Ham on 5 April. This was a new cover design showing Norwich Speedway in green against a yellow background.

Above right: The programme colours were reversed for the 1948 season with Norwich Speedway now being depicted in yellow on a green background. This is the cover for the first meeting of the 1948 season, a National League Second Division match against Wigan.

Right: A completely new cover design was introduced for the 1949 season. This is the cover for the first meeting of the season, a challenge match against 'The North', held on 9 April 1949.

Most of the programmes of this period carried a cartoon making some sort of pun on the name of the opposing team. The programme for the match against Newcastle, for example, showed a card game in which a Newcastle rider was holding the ace of diamonds (Newcastle's nickname was the Diamonds), but the Norwich rider was holding all the other aces. This one is from the match against Liverpool. Liverpool were known as the Chads. Chad was a famous wartime cartoon figure who was drawn looking over a fence saying 'Wot no eggs?' (or bread or meat or whatever it happened to be) to draw attention to wartime shortages.

On 21 May 1949 Norwich staged a Second Division Test match between England and Australia. The riders shown here lining up for the final heat include three Norwich riders. They are, from left to right: Junior Bainbridge (Glasgow and Australia), Phil Clarke (Norwich and England), Syd Littlewood (Norwich and Australia), Paddy Mills (Norwich and England).

The Australian Alec Hunter came to this country in 1949 and immediately joined Norwich. His first season was not a great success and he finished it with an average of 2.79. However he quickly showed some improvement and by 1951 was scoring at 6.58. He remained with the Stars until 1953.

The Australian Syd Littlewood began his career in Melbourne where he was spotted by Max Grosskreutz who signed him up for Norwich. He had one season in Stars' colours in 1938, and then returned to the Firs in 1947 in exchange for Wilf Jay, having ridden for Newcastle in 1946. He remained with the Stars until 1950, averaging around 4 to 5 per match.

Signed from West Ham for £250, Aussie Powell only had a couple of seasons at Norwich in 1947 and 1948.
Unfortunately his second season was cut short by injury just at the time when he was beginning to settle down and score well. He moved on to become manager at Rayleigh, where he trained riders such as Pat Clarke and Jack Unstead.

An action shot from the late 1940s showing Paddy Mills leading Newcastle's Hodgson brothers.

Junior Dennis Nelson taking part in Paddy Mills Training School in January 1949.

Paddy Mills Training School juniors in 1948/49. Mills is on the far left wearing the glasses. Next to him is Skid Parrish. Fourth from the right in the line-up is Malcolm Flood, one of the school's most impressive discoveries.

five

The Fred Evans Years, 1950-1954

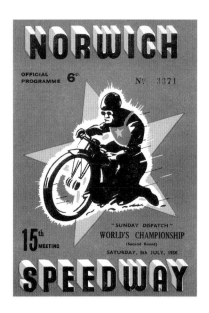

Above: The programme cover from the second round of the World Championship held at Norwich on 8 July 1950.

Above right: A page of Norwich riders' autographs from 1950. From the top: Phil Clarke, Bob Leverenz, Syd Littlewood, Johnny Davies, Alec Hunter, Ted Bravery.

Bob Leverenz, left and Phil Clarke, right, Norwich's top two riders of 1950, the year Norwich finally won the Second Division title. Clarke averaged 9.28 and Leverenz 8.25.

Bob Leverenz, shown here in Australian colours, joined Norwich in 1949 and remained with the team until 1952. In 1951 he averaged over 10 points per match, helping the Stars gain promotion to the First Division. The higher standard did not faze him and he again finished the 1952 season with a 10-point average. The only other riders to perform this feat were Jack Young and Ronnie Moore, two of the greatest riders of all time. Unfortunately Leverenz had to leave before the season was over and he never returned to this country to race.

Phil Basey, one of the Firs' backroom boys without whom speedway could not operate. He started as a programme seller just after the Second World War, graduating to the track staff and eventually to tractor driver. He remained as driver until Norwich's closure in 1964.

Fred Rogers was born in Sheffield and started his career riding at a number of northern tracks, including Sheffield, Bradford and Newcastle. He signed for Norwich in 1948 and became a very popular team man. He stayed with the Stars until 1954, leaving for Belle Vue at the end of the season.

Rogers was always a trier, and although he was never a world-beater he could be relied on to turn in a match-winning 6 or 7 points practically every time. He is shown here leading West Ham's Howdy Byford and Wally Green in a match at Custom House.

Right: Johnny Davies joined Norwich in 1949 and remained with the Stars until 1951. Unfortunately his last season was ended prematurely following a bad crash.

Below: Johnny Davies in action against West Ham as he tries to go round Howdy Byford.

Opposite above: Action from the 1952 league match against Birmingham, as Jack Freeman leads Birmingham's Swedish star Dan Forsberg.

Opposite below: This photograph shows, from left to right, Phil Clarke, Johnny Davies and Ted Bravery trying out the new Ipswich track on its first practice day in October 1950. Clarke set the fastest time of the afternoon at 72.2 seconds.

Right: Bill Codling was born in Norwich in 1927. He began his racing career at Yarmouth in 1948 and showed such promise that he was moved to Norwich in 1949. He remained with the Stars until 1954.

Below: Action from heat one of the match against Belle Vue on 7 August 1952. From left to right: Paddy Mills, Ron Johnston, Jack Parker. Parker was the track-record holder at the Firs at this time.

Opposite above: The 1950 Norwich team. From left to right: Phil Clarke, Jack Freeman, Johnny Davies, Fred Rogers, Syd Littlewood, Paddy Mills (on bike), Ted Bravery, Alec Hunter.

Opposite below: The 1951 Norwich team. From left to right: Fred Evans, Bill Codling, Paddy Mills, Johnny Davies, Jack Freeman, Phil Clarke (on bike), Fred Pawson, Bob Leverenz, Fred Rogers, Trevor Davies.

Right: Fred Pawson started his speedway career as a mechanic at Eastbourne in 1947. After practising at Rye House he was signed by Harringay in 1948. He moved to Norwich in 1951, coming straight in with a near-6-point average. On promotion to the First Division his average dropped to around 3 or 4 per match, but he remained in the reserve position until 1954.

Keihn Berthelsen (left) and Fred Pawson (right). Berthelsen rode nine times for Norwich in 1952, averaging 1.6.

Left: Bill Gilbert was spotted by Wembley manager Alec Jackson at the Rye House training school in 1945, and signed up for the famous Lions. He improved steadily, and in 1948 was chosen to ride for England against Australia in the fourth Test match, scoring 13 points. Later that year he came fourth in the British Riders' Championship. In 1949 he was Wembley's top scorer in a star-studded team that included the World Champion Tommy Price, Split Waterman, Bill Kitchen and Freddie Williams. Suddenly, at the end of the 1950 season, he announced his retirement.

Below: At the start of the 1952 season, Gilbert was approached by Fred Evans with a view to making a comeback for Norwich. Gilbert agreed and continued as though he had not been away from the sport. He finished the season as the Stars' top scorer. But, once again, at the end of the season, he announced his retirement, and this time he never came back.

Above left: Lionel Watling began his career at Tamworth in 1948 and signed for Norwich in 1952. He rode ten times for the Stars, averaging 3.6.

Above right: Ray Moore also began his career at the Rye House training track and was signed up by New Cross in 1947. He transferred to Norwich in 1952, but, although he had been an England international, he was not a great success, averaging just 1.1 from thirteen matches.

Harry Blanchflower (2nd from left in this photograph) was the man responsible for maintaining the Firs' reputation as one of the finest-prepared tracks in the country. Not only did he look after the track from 1947 until just before its closure, but among other things, he also kept the stadium clean, hung up the riders' race jackets and locked up after the night's racing. He was well respected by all riders, home and visiting, and was the very embodiment of the true Stars' spirit.

Left: Phil Clarke first rode for the Stars as a twenty-four-year-old in 1947. He quickly became one of Norwich's top riders and was appointed captain in 1951. He qualified for the World Championship final in 1955 and remained with the team until his retirement at the end of the 1959 season, having spent the whole of his racing career with one club. In all, he rode 309 matches for the Stars, scoring 2162 points, both club records.

Below: Phil Clarke receiving the Supporters' Trophy at the end of the 1950 season, the year Norwich won the Second Division.

Right: Billy Bales began his racing career as a cycle speedway star for the Hellesden Harriers on a track at the back of the Firs Stadium car park. In 1948 he graduated to the real thing with a second half at Yarmouth. After just this one outing he was put into the Yarmouth team as reserve the following week. He finished the meeting as joint-top scorer with 10 points. He soon became Yarmouth's top rider, but his career was interrupted when he was called up to the RAF.

Below: On his return to full-time civilian life in 1952, Bales was promoted to the Norwich team. His first match in the First Division, against Bradford, resulted in a maximum. His spectacular style made him a firm favourite with the Norwich supporters and he repaid their faith by remaining one of the National League's leading riders throughout the rest of his career with Norwich, which lasted until the Firs closed in 1964.

Left: This is a photograph of Bales taken at the Test match between Scotland and England raced at Glasgow White City on 24 August 1949. Bales was Norman Parker's partner and between them they scored 21 points, Bales contributing 8. Bales went on to represent his country many times over the next twenty years. In all, Bales represented Norwich in 245 matches, second only to Phil Clarke, scoring a total of 1580 points. He qualified for one World Championship final in 1955.

Below: The 1952 Norwich team. From left to right, back row: Fred Rogers, Jack Freeman, Phil Clarke, Bill Codling, Bill Gilbert, Fred Evans. Front row: Billy Bales, Bob Leverenz, Fred Pawson.

Above left: Merv Neil arrived in England in 1953 from his native New Zealand, where he had shot up the rankings over the 1952/53 season. He joined Norwich and turned in a useful 5.33 average. The following year he improved by over 1 point per match, scoring a maximum against West Ham on 26 June.

Above right: Trevor Davies was another rider to begin his career at Rye House. He was signed up by West Ham and put into their junior team in 1949. In 1951 he came to Norwich, but he always struggled and never got above the reserve berth.

A Norwich Speedway Supporters' Club card from 1951/52. There were three supporters' clubrooms where dances were held on Tuesdays, Thursdays and Saturdays.

CLUB NIGHTS
Tuesday, Thursday
and all race nights

★ ★ ★

DANCING
FOOTBALL
DARTS
BILLIARDS
SNOOKER
TABLE TENNIS
FISHING
NETBALL
CYCLE SPEEDWAY

NORWICH SPEEDWAY SUPPORTERS CLUB

1951-52

Membership Card

The 1953 Norwich team. From left to right, back row: Roy Craighead, Aub Lawson, Fred Evans, Fred Rogers, Cyril Roger. Front row: Fred Pawson, Billy Bales, Merv Neil, Phil Clarke.

The 1954 Norwich team. From left to right: Billy Bales, Fred Evans, Bob Oakley, Fred Brand, Phil Clarke, Cyril Roger (on bike), Fred Pawson, Merv Neil, Fred Rogers.

Right: In 1953, Norwich was chosen to hold a full Test match between England and Australia for the first time. This is the programme cover for the match.

Below: The local newspaper, the *Eastern Evening News*, made the Test match their front-page lead. The crowd was estimated at between 20,000 and 25,000.

NORWICH SPEEDWAY
HOLT ROAD, NORWICH　　　　'Phone : Norwich 26002

First
Official Test Match

ENGLAND

— *versus* —

AUSTRALIA

Saturday, 20th June, 1953

Meeting No.
12　　9ᴰ　SOUVENIR PROGRAMME　9ᴰ　Nº　5618

The right of admission to this Stadium is reserved.

Light-up—10.22 p.m.
Weather—Page 7
Wireless—Page 5

Eastern Evening News

SPEEDWAY SPECIAL

No. 21,959—Three Halfpence　　　　Saturday, June 20, 1953

'SELL OUT' AT THE FIRS TONIGHT

Last-minute demands for Test tickets flood in

CALM BEFORE STORM

Turn to centre pages for—

England's Prospects
Action Studies
Pen Pictures
Test History

STARS' MANAGER HOLDS ENGLAND REINS TONIGHT

The progress of the English Test team this evening will be guided by the manager of the Norwich track, Fred Evans. He will be bringing a long experience of the sport to bear on the subject and his knowledge of the track at the Firs can prove of invaluable assistance if any changes are needed in his team during the match.

Manager Evans has been with Norwich since March 1st, 1950, when he was appointed to succeed Dick Wise who had moved from Norfolk to the Birmingham Division II track at Cradley Heath. Evans came to Norwich following a spell of over ten years in the Army in which he attained the rank of major.

A native of Shropshire, he has been connected with speedway since 1933, when at the age of 21, he was introduced to the administrative side of the sport under the late Tom Bradbury, one of the pioneers of speedway in England. Within 12 months Evans was manager at Hall Green, Birmingham, and in 1935 he took over the reins at Hackney Wick.

In 1937, Evans was also associated with the old Nottingham track and on the Continent he ran meetings at the Buffalo Stadium in Paris.

The three seasons he has spent with Norwich have been years of ups and ...

SPEEDWAY supporters from all over the country—one hardy group has even made the long journey from Wales—have been converging on Norwich today for this evening's Test match between England and Australia.

All was tranquility at the stadium early this afternoon. But for the odd cars, the owners of which were calling for tickets, the car parks were empty. The grandstand and terraces where tonight there will be 25,000 cheering people, were bare, quiet. The track looked in perfect condition, and two groundsmen were busy sprinkling sections of it.

Autograph Hunters

Most interest in what little activity there was came from a group of youngsters who, armed with autograph books and pencils, were awaiting the arrival of their speed heroes.

No single telephone in Norwich has been more in demand today than that in the office of assistant manager, Frank Wilson. A reporter who called at the stadium early in the afternoon was informed that during the morning the staff had been swamped with enquiries for tickets. "This is going to be a sell out," he was told, and, as if to endorse this view, calls were coming in at the rate of about one a minute while he was there.

An Optimist

There was one optimist who thought he could collect his tickets at 2.15 p.m., and another caller from King's Lynn explained that he did not leave work until 5 p.m. but hoped to get to the track in time if only tickets could be reserved.

The earliest of the visiting riders to ...

The England Test squad for the match held on 20 June. From left to right, back row: Split Waterman, Arthur Forrest, Fred Evans (manager), Alan Hunt, Ken Sharples. Front row: Billy Bales, Fred Rogers, Brian Crutcher, Freddie Williams.

The Australia Test squad for the same match. From left to right, back row: Arthur Payne, Keith Gurtner, Arthur Simcock, Jack Young, Aub Lawson. Front row: Johnny Chamberlain, Ronnie Moore, Peter Moore, Jack Biggs.

Home star Billy Bales leads Split Waterman, Aub Lawson and Arthur Payne in this action shot from the Test match.

Another view of Bales in typically full action during the Test match. Bales top-scored for England, but he was unable to stop England losing 62-46.

Left: Cyril Roger arrived at Norwich midway through the 1953 season. He had been New Cross's top rider since 1949 but, when the club folded in mid-season, he moved on to Norwich. Unfortunately, he was unable to recapture the form that had made him one of England's top riders in the early 1950s. For the three years that he remained with the club he averaged around the 7.5 mark. He returned in 1959 for a further season once again averaging just over 7 per match. He qualified for the World Championship twice as a Norwich rider, both times coming last having scored no points.

Below: Cyril Roger leads Howdy Byford and Fred Brand in the National League match against West Ham on 26 June 1954.

Cyril Roger relaxing off duty.

A photograph taken during the 1953 Supporters' Club social. At the back, from left to right are: Roy Craighead, Fred Pawson, Barry East, Aub Lawson, Roy Blanchflower, Merv Neil, Wilf Lucy, Phil Clarke. Alec Hunter is sitting at the table on the right.

Bob Oakley's first acquaintance with speedway was at Wimbledon and New Cross just after the Second World War. Under the guidance of Mike Erskine, he moved down to Third Division Southampton to get more experience. He was so successful that he was appointed Saints' captain in 1949. He transferred to Wembley in 1950. In 1952 he finished third in the World Championship. He came to Norwich in 1954 but only stayed one season – starting well but fading as the season continued, dropping down to reserve. Ironically he scored his only maximum of the season from the reserve berth against Birmingham.

Fred Rogers and Merv Neil take a 5-1 at Wembley in 1954.

Left: Barry East, a junior rider with Norwich from 1952 to 1954.

Below: Norwich Speedways-headed notepaper in the Fred Evans era. The heading is green on yellow and the typeface is green. This letter dates from 1952.

Norwich Speedways LIMITED

DIRECTORS
E. HOWARD MANAGING
C. H. SUTTON

MANAGER: MAJOR F. L. EVANS, T.D.
DEPUTY MANAGER: F. A. WILSON

THE FIRS STADIUM
HOLT ROAD · NORWICH
TELEPHONE: NORWICH 26002

25th April 1952.

Gdsn G. Cockaday,
H.Q. Company,
Guards Training Btn,
Pirbright Camp,
WOKING, Surrey.

Dear Sir,

Thanks for your letter of the 19th inst regarding the match race meetings between Bob Leverenz and Jack Young.

The reason for their meetings on neutral tracks was the fact that both Edinburgh and ourselves raced on a Saturday night, and could not be spared by either track, when their teams were engaged in League matches.

Yours faithfully,
Norwich Speedways Ltd.

Fred Evans

Manager.

Left: In 1952 the programme cover was redesigned yet again. This is the first programme showing the new design, and was for the opening meeting of the 1952 season, the Easter Cup, held on 12 April. This design stayed until the end in 1964.

Opposite above: The Lady Mayor of Norwich presents the 1950 Second Division Trophy to Norwich. From left to right, back row: Johnny Davies, Bill Codling, Fred Rogers, Jack Freeman. Front row: Paddy Mills, the Mayor, -?-, Phil Clarke, Fred Evans, Ernie Howard, Ted Bravery.

Opposite below: The Mayor presents Paddy Mills with his individual medal at the same ceremony.

Fred Evans and Mrs Bilner present the Firs Trophy and the Bilner Cup to Bill Gilbert on 4 October 1952.

Above left: Tich Read first turned out for Norwich in 1950 as a junior. He returned to Norwich for their last season in 1964, winning the very last meeting at the Firs when he took the Supporters' Trophy.

Above right: Roy Craighead first practised speedway alongside Bill Gilbert at Rye House. Like Gilbert, he was signed up by Wembley. He later moved on to Southampton and in 1953 came to Norwich. He was not a great success, riding in just six matches as reserve.

The second leg of the 1954 National Trophy final between Norwich and Wembley at the Firs. From left to right: Merv Neil, Brian Crutcher, Eric Williams, Aub Lawson. The track was very wet and slippery. Wembley won both legs to take the Trophy by 123 points to 92.

To compensate for the loss of Gilbert and Leverenz, Fred Evans pulled off a major coup before the 1953 season by signing up Aub Lawson. In the late 1940s and early 1950s, West Ham's Australian star had been one of the top riders in the world. He retired from British racing at the end of 1951. He is seen here signing forms for Norwich.

Above: As well as being one of the best riders in the world, Lawson was also one of the most spectacular, and was instantly recognisable as he flew round the track with his chequered scarf streaming out behind him. Although his first year in Stars colours was average by his own standards, he seemed to improve with age.

Left: He stayed with the Stars until 1960, by which time he was forty-four years of age. In his last year he was still averaging 9.97.

His greatest moment individually came in 1958 when he came third in the World Championship, behind Barry Briggs and teammate Ove Fundin. It was a remarkable achievement. To give some idea of how remarkable it was, it must be remembered that the mid-1950s to the mid-1960s was the period dominated by the 'Big Five' (Ove Fundin, Ronnie Moore, Barry Briggs, Peter Craven and Bjorn Knutsson). In the nine years between 1955 and 1963 they finished in the first three of the World Championship no less than twenty-four out of twenty-seven times. Their dominance was broken only by Arthur Forrest, Gote Nordin and Aub Lawson. Lawson was forty-two at the time he came third.

Right: Lawson was also noted for being a gentleman on the track and was commended by ACU officials on more than one occasion. He is seen here surrounded by his family.

Left: Lawson's two sons, Lionel and John. John was the team mascot.

Aub Lawson tries to get inside Cyril Brine of Wimbledon in the match against Wimbledon on 5 June 1954. Cyril Roger is in third place.

Les Mullins, on the right of this picture, began as a junior rider with Norwich in the late 1940s. Unfortunately, a bad crash at Yarmouth put paid to his riding career, so he joined Wilf Lucy as a mechanic in Norwich's workshop. When Lucy left to join Belle Vue, Mullins became chief mechanic. When Fundin joined the team, Mullins became his personal mechanic and worked with him throughout his career at Norwich, helping him to four world titles.

six

The Gordon Parkins Years,
1955-1964

The 1955 Norwich team. From left to right, back row: Harry Edwards, Fred Brand, Gordon Parkins, Cyril Roger, Phil Clarke, Malcolm Flood. Front row: Don Lawson, Aub Lawson, Ove Fundin, Billy Bales.

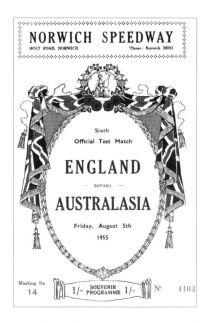

Above left: The programme cover for the England *v.* Australasia Test match held on 5 August 1955 at Norwich.

Above right: Two Norwich riders, Aub Lawson and Billy Bales, were appointed captain of their respective sides. Here they shake hands before the match.

The England team for the match. From left to right, back row: Brian Crutcher, Ken Middleditch, Cyril Roger, Phil Clarke, Ron How. Front row: Arthur Forrest, Billy Bales (on bike), Arthur Wright.

The Australasian team for the match. From left to right: Peter Clarke, Jack Geran, Peter Moore, Arthur Simcock (manager), Barry Briggs, Bob Duckworth, Ron Johnston, Jack Young. On the bike in the front is Aub Lawson.

In all, there were four Norwich riders in the match. From left to right: Phil Clarke, Aub Lawson, Billy Bales, Cyril Roger.

Action from the match with Lawson leading Middleditch and Bales. England won the match by 57 points to 51. Bales was England's top scorer with 13 points. Clarke scored 7 and Roger 5, while Lawson scored 4 for Australasia.

Right: The programme cover for the National Trophy final second leg, held at the Firs on 17 September 1955.

Below: Norwich's victory in the 1955 National Trophy gave them their first senior trophy. Pictured on the tractor at the presentation are Les Mullins, Reg Trott, Don Lawson and Aub Lawson.

Above: An image from the Norwich *v.* West Ham National League match held on 16 July 1955. From left to right: Gerry Hussey, Fred Brand, Bert Roger, Ove Fundin.

Right: Peter Atkins appeared for the Stars in 1956, scoring 20 points from ten matches.

Above: Malcolm and Maurice Flood. Malcolm was discovered through the Paddy Mills Training School. He was in and out of the Norwich team throughout the early 1950s. He tragically lost his life in a crash at Poole in April 1956.

Left: Derek Strutt was another to graduate from the cycle-speedway ranks. He first rode real speedway at Norwich in 1955, and by 1956 was a team regular. He remained with the Stars until 1962.

As a novice at Norwich in the late 1940s, Fred Brand was farmed out to Yarmouth, where he soon became the Bloaters' top rider, finishing up as their leading points-scorer of all time. In 1954 he moved back to Norwich and was far from outclassed in the First Division, playing a big part in the Stars' move up the table from seventh to fourth. He also qualified for the World Championship final that year, scoring 7 points to finish in seventh place. He stayed with Norwich until 1956.

Geoff Pymar returned to the Firs in 1956, twenty-four years after riding in the original unofficial 1932 Norwich team. He stayed with the Stars in 1957 before moving on again. He eventually retired at the end of the 1962 season, having had one of the longest careers in speedway history.

Harry Edwards spent four years in a Japanese prisoner-of-war camp before returning home to take up speedway. Another Rye House discovery, he made his team debut for Walthamstow in 1949. He signed for Norwich in 1955 and remained with the Stars until 1961.

Fred Brand and Harry Edwards lead Arthur Duncan of Birmingham in the match on 2 June 1956.

Harry Edwards and Gerry Hussey lead Poole's Terry Small in the match held on 30 June 1956.

Peter Atkins leads Poole's Norman Strachan in the same match.

Opposite above: The 1956 Norwich team. From left to right, back row: Harry Edwards, Geoff Pymar, Gordon Parkins, Ove Fundin, Fred Brand, Phil Clarke. Front row: Billy Bales, Aub Lawson (on bike), Reg Trott.

Opposite below: The 1957 Norwich team. From left to right, back row: Phil Clarke, Harry Edwards, Gordon Parkins, Aub Lawson, Ove Fundin, Wal Morton. Front row: Geoff Pymar, John Lawson (mascot), Billy Bales.

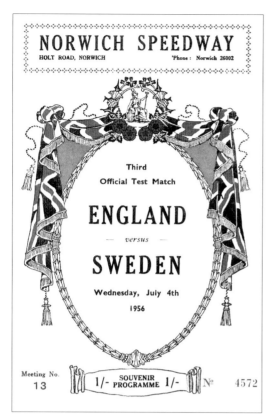

The programme cover from the England *v.* Sweden Test match held at the Firs on 4 July 1956.

The Swedish team line-up for the match. In the far background is the Firs pub.

Arthur South, Lord Mayor of Norwich, meets Ove Fundin before the start of the match. Dan Forsberg is between the Mayor and Fundin.

Fundin leads Ken McKinlay and Brian Crutcher in heat six of the match. This was the only race McKinlay lost all night. England won the match 66–42. Fundin scored 15 points for Sweden.

Derek Strutt in action against Southampton on 21 July 1957.

Aub Lawson and Ove Fundin take the lead against Belle Vue on 25 July 1956.

Right: The programme cover from the Astorias Trophy meeting held on 21 April 1956. The trophy was won by Ove Fundin, who scored 14 points, from Brian Crutcher on 13. Strangely enough they dropped their points in the same heat, when Phil Clarke beat both of them.

Below: Fundin receives the Astorias Trophy from Celia Tomlin.

Above left: The programme cover for Buck Ryan's International Wild West Rodeo meeting held on 21 May 1956, which included a challenge match between Norwich Starlets and Rye House. In spite of a 15-point maximum from Peter Atkins, the Starlets lost 44-40.

Above right: Wal Morton leads Ipswich's Otto Holoubeck, 11 May 1957.

Right: Gerry Hussey was an overnight sensation when he signed up as a junior for West Ham in 1954. In his first match he scored 7 points from the reserve spot. He came to Norwich in 1956, scoring 63 points from ten matches and qualifying for the World Championship final. He then moved on to Leicester. He was tragically killed while racing midget cars in Australia in March 1959.

Opposite above: Gerry Hussey relaxing in the bath after a hard meeting.

Opposite below: Gerry Hussey in action against Poole on 30 June 1956.

Right: Wal Morton in 1957, the third time he had ridden for Norwich, following his pre-war appearances and his spell in 1948. Like Pymar, Morton continued riding until well into the 1960s, finally retiring in 1963, following a spell with Hackney, as the last pre-war rider still to be holding down a regular team place.

Below: Billy Bales leads Ron How and Gerald Jackson in the match against Wimbledon on 1 June 1957.

NORWICH
SPEEDWAY

N° 2721

— *Programme* —

OF THE

C.T.S.
CONTINENTAL
TROPHY

SOUVENIR PROGRAMME Price 1/-

Left: The programme cover for the CTS Continental Trophy held on 26 June 1957.

Below: Action from the CTS Trophy meeting with Phil Clarke leading Jack Biggs and Harry Edwards.

A scene in the pits before the meeting. From left to right, back row: Peter Moore, Phil Clarke, Peo Soderman. Front row: Ken McKinlay, Bert Edwards, Peter Craven, Aub Lawson, Harry Edwards.

Norwich director Jack Thompson and his wife Phyllis present the winner of the meeting, Ove Fundin, with the CTS Trophy. The runner-up, Aub Lawson, is standing to the left.

The programme cover for the England *v.* Overseas Test match held on 17 July 1957. England won the match 59-48, with Bales and Clarke scoring 13 and 11 respectively for England, and Lawson and Fundin 7 and 5 for Overseas.

The programme cover for the Britannia Cup final match against Belle Vue on 7 August 1957. Although Norwich had drawn the first leg away at Hyde Road, they lost the home leg to give Belle Vue victory. To make matters worse, Craven also retained the Golden Helmet against Fundin's challenge.

From left to right: Dave Hankins, Billy Bales and John Lawson cheering on fellow Stars in a match at Southampton.

Three leading Stars from the 1956 season. From left to right: Gerry Hussey, Ove Fundin, Aub Lawson.

Right: A leading grass-track rider, Arne Hendriksen began his career in speedway at Wimbledon. He was given a trial at Norwich at the end of 1957 and gained a team place in 1958, but was injured in a match at Wimbledon. On his return to fitness he was loaned to Swindon.

Below: Harry Edwards (left) and his brother Bert (right). Bert was also a speedway rider who rode for Ipswich among others, but never rode for Norwich.

Left: The Australian Johnny Chamberlain had established himself in this country at Yarmouth. In 1958, after a move to Ipswich, he transferred to Norwich where he gave strong back-up support to Fundin, Lawson and Bales, and played a major part in what was the Stars' best season up to that time, as they finished runners-up in both the National League and the National Trophy.

Right: Chamberlain is said to be the smallest rider ever to race in speedway. But he was a 100 per cent trier who was always good value for money in any race he rode in. On 26 August 1961, during a Lions *v.* Kangaroos match, he went through the safety fence breaking both his wrists in one of the most spectacular crashes ever seen at the Firs. He never rode again. During his time with Norwich he was chosen to represent Australasia in two Test matches.

Right: Denis Newton was a protégé of former Norwich rider Aussie Powell. His first club was Cradley Heath, for whom he signed in 1950. He arrived at Norwich in 1958 by way of Wembley, St Austell and Oxford. He stayed until 1961.

Below: Dave Hankins receives the Malcolm Flood Junior Cup from Maurice Flood on 25 August 1956. Hankins was a product of the Norwich Training School. After a spell with Brafield, he was brought into the Norwich team in 1957 but was unable to maintain a team place.

Opposite above: The 1958 Norwich team. From left to right, back row: Reg Trott, Harry Edwards, Jack Norton, Ove Fundin. Front row: Phil Clarke, Aub Lawson, Billy Bales.

Opposite below: The 1959 Norwich team. From left to right: Phil Clarke, Billy Bales, Harry Edwards, Aub Lawson, Johnny Chamberlain, Reg Trott, Gordon Parkins, Cyril Roger, Ove Fundin.

Above: While riding for Yarmouth in 1959 and 1960, John Debbage had a few outings for Norwich, transferring full time in 1961. He remained a Star until the Firs closed, but never rose much above the reserve spot.

Left: Reg Trott first rode for Norwich on 17 September 1955 in the National Trophy final. He was appointed captain in 1961 following Aub Lawson's retirement. He remained captain until Norwich's closure. A steady if unspectacular rider, Trott could always be relied upon to shore up the middle order.

Above left: Former Wembley rider Jimmy Gooch joined the Stars in 1962, following the closure of New Cross at the end of the previous season. He slotted in immediately as the third-heat leader behind Fundin and Betts. He stayed for one more season.

Below left: Terry Betts joined Norwich as a seventeen-year-old in 1960. He rode in four matches that year and did not score a single point! He showed a bit more promise in 1961, but in 1962 he suddenly shot to stardom, a position he was to hold for over fifteen years. The turning point came on 14 July 1962 when, on a night that Fundin was to score a mere 4 points against Belle Vue, Betts weighed in with a 15-point maximum, including two victories over Peter Craven, who later that year would be crowned World Champion. Betts finished the season as the Stars' second-highest scorer, behind Fundin.

Opposite above: The 1960 Norwich team. From left to right, back row: Denis Newton, Derek Strutt, Ove Fundin, Gordon Parkins, Harry Edwards, Reg Trott. Front row: Johnny Chamberlain, Aub Lawson (on bike), Billy Bales.

Opposite below: The 1961 Norwich team. From left to right: Johnny Chamberlain, Denis Newton, Gordon Parkins, Reg Trott (on bike), Ove Fundin, John Debbage, Derek Strutt, Billy Bales.

The Swede Olle Nygren first rode for Norwich as a replacement for Ove Fundin in 1962, while the latter was out of action through injury. Parkins was so impressed with his form that he signed up him as a permanent team member the following year. Nygren breathed new life into the Stars as 1963 proved to be their best-ever season, winning the National Trophy for the second time and finishing runners-up in the National League.

Nygren had an unmistakable style and was one of the most exciting riders to watch. He had been a top-class rider since the early 1950s when he came over to this country to ride for Harringay. He remained with the Stars for their last season.

Right: Former Norfolk cycle-speedway champion Trevor Hedge joined the Stars in 1961. Although he didn't set the world alight at first he made good steady progress and showed great potential. By the time of the closure it was obvious he had the makings of a world-class star.

Below: Hedge's subsequent career led him to Hackney and Wimbledon, and to many international honours as he represented his country on many occasions. In 1970 he saved his country's honour in another way by being the only Englishman in the World Championship final. If he hadn't qualified it would have been the only year in the history of the World Championship without an English representative in the final.

Opposite above: The 1962 Norwich team. From left to right: Billy Bales, Terry Betts, John Debbage, Reg Trott (on bike), Gordon Parkins, Ove Fundin, Jimmy Gooch, Eric Williams.

Opposite below: The 1963 Norwich team. From left to right, back row: Olle Nygren, Gordon Parkins, Ove Fundin, Billy Bales. Front row: John Debbage, Jimmy Gooch, Reg Trott, Terry Betts.

Above: From left to right: Olle Nygren, Gote Nordin, Ove Fundin. Nygren and Nordin were called up for the Stars on a temporary basis in 1962 to replace the injured Fundin.

Right: Captain and star rider in Norwich's final year, 1964. Reg Trott (left) Ove Fundin (right).

Left: There is no doubt that Norwich's – and many would argue the world's – greatest rider of all time was Ove Fundin. This photograph was taken during his third meeting for Norwich away at West Ham on 12 July 1955, in which he scored 14 points. Fundin's first full season was in his home country, Sweden, in 1952. In 1954 he had his first ride at the Firs in the World Championship qualifying round, where he amazed everyone by scoring 13 points on a bike tied up with old bits of wire and string. He qualified for the World Championship final, where he still had just this one bike and no mechanic. Aub Lawson, who had been impressed by the youngster, arranged for a mechanic to help him.

Below: When Lawson saw Fundin again during the close season in Australia, he recommended to Norwich's new manager Gordon Parkins that he sign up this youngster immediately before another promoter got him. It was a move Lawson, Parkins and Norwich were never to regret. Fundin went on to dominate proceedings at the Firs until Norwich's closure in 1964.

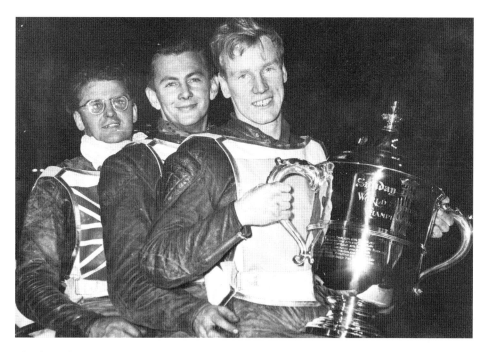

The first of Fundin's record-breaking five World Championship wins came in 1956. He is seen here holding the coveted trophy. Behind him are Ronnie Moore (who came second) and Arthur Forrest (third).

After finishing in the runner-up position for the next three years, Fundin again took the World Championship in 1960 following a season in which he had completely dominated the sport in Britain. Behind him on the tractor are Ronnie Moore (second) and Peter Craven (third).

Left: Fundin's success was instrumental in the FIM taking the World Championship final away from Wembley for the first time ever, and awarding it to Sweden the following year. It made no difference to Fundin as he once again took the title in Malmo. With Fundin on the podium are Bjorn Knutsson (left) and Gote Nordin (right).

Below: His final win as a Norwich rider came in 1963 when, back at Wembley, he took the title from Bjorn Knutsson and Barry Briggs. He was to win the title once more in 1967.

Right: As well as winning the World Championship four times as a Norwich rider, many other trophies came his way, including the British Match Race Championship, which he won on many occasions, and was the first foreign rider to do so. His contribution not only to Norwich speedway but to British and world speedway as a whole is incalculable.

Below: The 1964 Norwich team. From left to right: Billy Bales, Olle Nygren, Sandor Levai, Ove Fundin, Reg Trott (on bike), John Debbage, Trevor Hedge, Tich Read.

Left: The programme cover for the last-ever meeting at the Firs, signed by many of the riders who took part. Although the programme is dated 14 October, the meeting actually took place on 31 October as the original running was rained off.

Below: The Norwich Speedway Supporters' Club Dinner, 1961. What was so tragic about Norwich's closure was that right up until the end Norwich was one of the best-supported clubs in the country, and it wasn't through lack of support that the Firs closed. It was purely a business decision to maximise profits on the land.

Dancing to
THE CYRIL GLOVER SHOW BAND
Supported by
THE RIVERSIDE JAZZMEN (with Vivienne)

Your M.C.
Mr. TODD SLAUGHTER

MENU CARDS
presented by Morris Printing Co., Ltd.
Flowers: Mrs. S. Pulford

NORWICH SPEEDWAY
SUPPORTERS' CLUB
(Firs Stadium Limited)

★

Eighth Invitation

DINNER

★

Norwood Rooms, Norwich

Thursday, October 26th, 1961

Tuesday, March 3, 1964

FIRS STADIUM SOLD

Norfolk property company buys 14-acre site

BUT PLAN FOR HOUSES TURNED DOWN

NORWICH SPEEDWAYS LTD. HAVE SOLD THE FIRS STADIUM TO A PROPERTY DEVELOPMENT COMPANY, NORFOLK GARDEN ESTATES LTD.

The development company, headed by a former Norwich solicitor, Mr. L. B. Summers, planned to erect low-cost homes for 700 people on the 14-acre site, and make half of them available for letting.

The planning authority, however, has rejected the application.

Even if the application had been successful the land would not have been wanted for building and contracting until after the end of the coming speedway season, due to start on March 28th.

The position after that, however, remains obscure, for Norfolk Garden Estates Ltd. intend to appeal.

Mr. L. C. Goose, Clerk to St. Faith's and Aylsham R.D.C., said today the main reason for the refusal was that the application was contrary to the development plan.

THE Firs was a great speedway track in the early 1930's, and developed over the years into the greatest in that sport. Max Grosskreutz played a big part in the early days of the sport and enter the ace Dick Wise as manager and Mr. Ernest Howard as chairman of the board, guided the Stars through the boom years.

At this period crowds of 20,000 were not exceptional. Gates nowadays reach the 10,000 mark, and are usually around 6000.

The Norwich team entered the National League, Division II, in 1937, and were promoted to the First Division in 1951.

Among famous riders to visit the Norwich colours have been Bert Spencer, Paddy Mills, Bob Leverenz, Aub Lawson, and, of course, the reigning world champion, Ove Fundin.

Right: How the local paper announced the news that the Firs had been sold to a property company on 3 March 1964.

Below: A sad picture of the Firs during its demolition in 1965.

127

NORWICH RACEWAY

Good afternoon, ladies and gentlemen,

A very cordial welcome to Hevingham, the new Norwich Raceway.

For a dozen years, there have been strenuous attempts made to fill the void created by the disappearance from the local motor-cycling scene of the old Norwich Firs Stadium.

Today, you will be witnessing one of the first steps in the campaign to bring back League speedway racing to Norwich, traditionally regarded as one of THE centres for the sport.

This is the setting for racing to thrive again; a venue which provides the basis for amenities which will satisfy and even delight the thousands who have clamoured for such an arena, without infringing upon the sensibilities of those who for reasons of their own have blocked this and other proposed ventures.

It is wholly fitting that the Norwich Supporters' Club were invited to lend their patronage to the first meeting here, since their grass roots enthusiasm and determination has been one of the sustaining factors in a long fight.

We invite you, members of the public, to enjoy yourselves at this most convivial of family sports, and to demonstrate your support for our bid to put Norwich back on the sporting map.

Individual meetings, team matches, all fought out in the best spirit and in front of appreciative and enthusiastic fans — that's the recipe we have in mind.

Come ride with us !

SUNDAY, DECEMBER 5, 1976 at 1.45 p.m.

NORWICH SUPPORTERS' TROPHY

Admission by Programme

Postscript

One more meeting was held in Norwich at Hevingham on 5 December 1976. This was an unofficial meeting put on by Cyril Crane and Violet Littlechild. The idea was to demonstrate speedway to Norwich Council prior to asking planning permission to run twenty-four meetings in the 1977 season. Although 2,000 supporters turned out, the meeting ultimately proved to be a failure as the council refused permission.